D1824859

Top Cookbook Pick for Beer Lovers

Cooking with Beer is Made Easy with These 40 Recipes

By

Angel Burns

License Notices

This book or parts thereof might not be reproduced in any format for personal or commercial use without the written permission of the author. Possession and distribution of this book by any means without said permission is prohibited by law.

All content is for entertainment purposes and the author accepts no responsibility for any damages, commercially or personally, caused by following the content.

Table of Contents

Cooking with Beer

HHHHHHHHHHHHHHHHHHHHHHHHHHHHHHHHHHHHHHHH

Dips and Sides

HHHHHHHHHHHHHHHHHHHHHHHHHHHHHHHHHHH

Recipe 1: Mac n Beer Cheese

An adult take on an all-American favorite dish. Serve this beer-infused mac n cheese dish with pulled pork, sausages, meatloaf or chicken.

Yield: 10-12

Preparation Time: 35mins

Ingredient List:

- 1 (16 ounce) pack elbow macaroni
- ¼ cup butter
- 2 cloves garlic (peeled, minced)
- ¼ cup all-purpose flour
- 1 tablespoon ground mustard
- 1 teaspoon salt
- ¾ teaspoons pepper
- 2½ cups 2% milk
- ¾ cup amber beer
- ¼ cup heavy whipping cream
- 3 cups Cheddar cheese (shredded, divided)
- 2 cups Fontina cheese (shredded)
- 2 tablespoons Parmesan cheese (grated, divided)
- 2 tablespoons chives (minced)
- 5 strips of bacon (cooked, crumbled)

HHHHHHHHHHHHHHHHHHHHHHHHHHHHHHHHHHHHHHH

Instructions:

1. Cook the pasta according to the package instruction, until al dente. Drain.

2. In the meantime, in a Dutch oven, over moderate to high heat, heat the butter.

3. Add the garlic and cook while stirring for 60 seconds.

4. Stir in the flour followed by the mustard, salt, and pepper until silky smooth.

5. Gradually add, while whisking to combine, the milk, beer, and heavy cream. Bring to boil and cook while stirring for 2 minutes, or until the mixture is thickened.

6. Turn the heat down and stir in 2 cups of shredded Cheddar, the shredded Fontina cheese and 1 tablespoon of Parmesan.

7. Scatter with the chives.

8. Stir the cooked pasta into the sauce and transfer to a greased casserole dish of approximately 3 quart capacity.

9. Garnish with the remaining Cheddar and Parmesan.

10. Bake in an oven at 400 degrees F, uncovered for 15-20 minutes, or until heated through and golden.

11. Garnish with crumbled bacon and allow to stand for a few minutes before serving.

Recipe 2: Rice with Beer

Cooking rice in beer will give it a nutty flavor, and what's more, it will ensure its fluffy and non-sticky.

Yield: 6

Preparation Time: 30mins

Ingredient List:

- 2 tablespoons butter
- 1¼ cups rice (uncooked)
- 1 (12 ounce) bottle beer
- 1¼ cups water
- ½ teaspoons onion powder

HHHHHHHHHHHHHHHHHHHHHHHHHHHHHHHHHHHHHHH

Instructions:

1. Over moderate heat, melt the butter in a large frying pan.

2. Add the rice and cook until starting to brown for 4-5 minutes.

3. Add the beer along with the water and onion powder.

4. Cover the pan and simmer until the liquid is absorbed, for approximately 20-25 minutes.

Recipe 3: Drunken Beans

Good to go in less than half an hour, these frijoles borrochos or drunken beans are guaranteed to make a good meal, great.

Yield: 6-8

Preparation Time: 25mins

Ingredient List:

- 4 slices raw bacon (diced)
- 1 small white onion (peeled, thinly sliced)
- 1 jalapeno (stemmed, seeded, diced)
- 4 garlic cloves (peeled, finely chopped)
- 1 (12 ounce) can Mexican beer
- 4 (15 ounce) cans pinto beans (rinsed, drained)
- 1 tablespoon brown sugar
- 1 teaspoon oregano
- 1 teaspoon chili powder
- 1 teaspoon salt
- ½ teaspoons cumin
- 1 tablespoon freshly squeezed lime juice
- ¼ cup fresh cilantro (chopped)

HHHHHHHHHHHHHHHHHHHHHHHHHHHHHHHHHHHH

Instructions:

1. Over moderate to high heat, cook the bacon in a frying pan. Cook until crisp while occasionally stirring.

2. With a slotted spoon, remove the bacon from the pan and transfer to a kitchen paper towel lined plate. Set to one side.

3. In the meantime, discard all but 1 tablespoon of bacon grease in the pan.

4. Add the onion followed by the jalapeno and fry for 4-5 minutes, until the onion is translucent and softened.

5. Add the garlic and sauté for another couple of minutes until fragrant.

6. Pour in the beer and add the beans followed by the brown sugar, oregano, chili powder, salt, and cumin, stirring to combine.

7. Continue to cook until the beans come to a simmer.

8. Turn the heat down to moderate to low and continue to simmer, uncovered for approximately 15 minutes.

9. When you are ready to serve, stir in the bacon along with the fresh lime juice.

10. Serve the beans garnished with cilantro.

Recipe 4: Beer Biscuit Squares

Bake up a batch of light and fluffy biscuits to enjoy with hummus, ham, jam, and jellies. Perfect as a side or for brunch.

Yield: 8-10

Preparation Time:

Ingredient List:

- 2 cups all-purpose flour
- 2 teaspoons baking powder
- ¼ teaspoons bicarb soda
- 1 tablespoon sugar
- ¼ teaspoons salt
- 6 tablespoons butter (melted, divided)
- 1 cup beer
- Nonstick baking spray

HHHHHHHHHHHHHHHHHHHHHHHHHHHHHHHHHHHHH

Instructions:

1. Preheat the main oven to 375 degrees F.

2. In a bowl, whisk the flour with the baking powder, bicarb, sugar and salt and mix until well combined.

3. Add 5 tablespoons of melted butter followed by the beer and with a spoon, mix.

4. Turn the mixture out onto a clean, floured worktop.

5. Pat or roll the dough out and with a square biscuit cutter, cut into biscuits.

6. Lightly spritz a baking sheet with nonstick spray and arrange the biscuits on the sheet.

7. Bake in the oven for 20 minutes.

8. Remove the biscuits from the oven and brush with the remaining melted butter.

9. Place the biscuits under your broiler for 2-3 minutes.

10. Set to one side to cool and serve.

Recipe 5: Warm Potato Salad with Beer Dressing

Serve this versatile and tasty potato salad with burgers, hot dogs or grilled meats.

Yield: 8-10

Preparation Time: 1hour 10mins

Ingredient List:

Beer Dressing:

- Olive oil
- 1 small yellow onion (peeled, finely chopped)
- 1 clove garlic (peeled, finely chopped)
- 1 (12 ounce) bottle German lager
- 4 tablespoons cider vinegar
- ½ teaspoons sugar
- 1 tablespoon Dijon mustard
- Salt and pepper

Potato Salad:

- 2½ pounds red potatoes
- 1 small red onion (peeled, finely chopped)
- 1 small yellow onion (peeled, finely chopped)
- ¼ cup parsley (finely chopped)
- 6 bacon strips (cooked no crispy, drained, chopped)
- 2 hard-boiled eggs (peeled, chopped)
- Chives (chopped, to garnish)
- Salt and pepper
- Fresh chives (to serve)

HHHHHHHHHHHHHHHHHHHHHHHHHHHHHHHHHH

Instructions:

1. First, prepare the beer dressing. Over moderate heat, heat olive oil in a pan.

2. Add the onion and garlic and cook until softened.

3. Pour in the lager and add the vinegar and sugar, boiling for 5 minutes.

4. Transfer the mixture along with the mustard to a blender and process, At the same time gradually add 5 tablespoons of oil and blend to thicken.

5. Season and add the dressing to the salad, when instructed.

6. To prepare the salad.

7. Add the potatoes to a large pot of boiling salted water and cook until just fork tender, 20-30 minutes.

8. Remove the potatoes from the pot and allow to cool for 3-4 minutes before slicing into ¼" round pieces.

9. Gently stir in the onions, followed by the parsley, chopped bacon, and eggs. Add the beer dressing, taking care not to smash the potatoes into small pieces.

10. Season with salt and pepper.

11. Garnish with chives and serve warm.

Recipe 6: Beer Poached Mushrooms

Delectable buttery mushrooms soak up the beer's malty flavor to create the best-ever side order.

Yield: 4

Preparation Time: 40mins

Ingredient List:

- 3 tablespoons butter
- 2 garlic cloves (peeled, minced)
- 8 ounces each of white mushrooms and cremini mushrooms (wiped cleaned, cut in half)
- 1 cup beer
- 1 tablespoon fresh oregano (chopped)
- Kosher salt and black pepper
- Crusty French bread (to serve)

HHHHHHHHHHHHHHHHHHHHHHHHHHHHHHHHHHHHH

Instructions:

1. Over moderate heat, in a skillet, melt the butter.

2. Add the garlic to the skillet and simmer, while stirring, until fragrant, for 30 seconds. Take care not to brown the garlic.

3. Add the mushrooms, tossing to coat evenly in the butter and garlic.

4. Gradually pour in the beer and on moderate to low heat, bring to simmer.

5. Add the oregano and season.

6. Poach the mushrooms in the beer, while occasionally stirring for 25-30 minutes.

7. Garnish with oregano and serve with crusty French bread.

Recipe 7: Porter Collard Greens

Like greens? Then you will love the flavor of fresh collard greens combined with bacon and rich porter.

Yield: 6-8

Preparation Time: 1hour 40mins

Ingredient List:

- 1 pound collard greens
- 2 cups water
- 1 teaspoon salt
- ¼ pound double smoked bacon (cut into cubes)
- 12 ounces British porter or stout

HHHHHHHHHHHHHHHHHHHHHHHHHHHHHHHHHHHHH

Instructions:

1. Clean the greens and chop them 4-5 times. Discard the bottom stems. Combine the water with the salt, cubes of bacon and porter in a large pot.

2. Bring water to boil and add the collard greens. Reduce to a simmer and cook, while covered for 1½ hours while occasionally mixing. The liquid may not cover the contents immediately but as soon as the veggies begin to steam they will sink into the liquid.

3. Sieve and serve.

Recipe 8: Beer Salsa Dip

This dip is perfect for game-night. Its thin consistency and texture is great to serve in taco boat shells.

Yield:

Preparation Time: 5mins

Ingredient List:

- 3 tomatoes (chopped)
- 1 jalapeno (stem removed)
- 1 small onion (peeled, chopped)
- Freshly squeezed juice of ½ lime
- ½ teaspoons garlic (peeled, minced)
- ¼ cup beer
- Salt
- Taco boat shells (to serve)

HHHHHHHHHHHHHHHHHHHHHHHHHHHHHHHHHHHH

Instructions:

1. Add the tomatoes, jalapeno, onion, juice, garlic, and beer to a food blender and process to a smooth consistency.

2. Taste and season.

3. Serve chilled with taco boat shells.

Recipe 9: Malty Beer Gravy

Beef and onion gravy is delicious served with sausages, burgers, mushrooms and creamy mash.

Yield: 4-6

Preparation Time: 20mins

Ingredient List:

- 4 tablespoons unsalted butter
- ¼ cup all-purpose flour
- 1 yellow onion (peeled, thinly sliced)
- 2 cloves garlic (peeled, minced)
- 2 cups beef stock
- 2 cups dark malty beer
- Salt

HHHHHHHHHHHHHHHHHHHHHHHHHHHHHHHHHHHHH

Instructions:

1. In a pan over moderate to high heat, melt the butter.

2. Add the flour, whisking until silky smooth.

3. Add the onion along with the garlic and cook for 5 minutes, until softened.

4. Pour in the stock and the beer and bring to boil, while constantly stirring for 7-10 minutes, until thickened.

5. Remove from the heat and season.

Recipe 10: Cajun Seasoned Fries in Beer Batter

Enjoy a taste of the Deep South with these Cajun seasoned, golden, crispy fries.

Yield: 4-6

Preparation Time: 8hours 22mins

Ingredient List:

- 2 pounds russet potatoes
- 2 cups all-purpose flour
- 1 tablespoon Cajun spice
- 2 teaspoons garlic salt
- 2 teaspoons onion powder
- 2 teaspoons paprika
- 2 teaspoons kosher salt
- 1 teaspoon ground black pepper
- 1 cup lager beer
- Peanut oil (to fry)

HHHHHHHHHHHHHHHHHHHHHHHHHHHHHHHHHHHH

Instructions:

1. Cut the unpeeled potatoes across their length into ¼"
slices. Next, cut the slices into ¼" sticks. Transfer the slices
to an ice bath and allow to soak for between 2-8 hours. This
will help to remove any starch.

2. In a bowl, combine the flour with the Cajun spices, garlic
salt, onion powder, paprika, salt, pepper, and beer to form a
thick pancake batter consistency. Add additional beer if
needed.

3. Evenly divide the batter between 2 mixing bowls.

4. Add the potatoes to one of the mixing bowls and toss to
coat evenly.

5. Fill a large enamel pot with peanut oil, fill to
approximately 3".

6. Heat the oil over moderate to high heat, to 325 degrees F.

7. In a few batches, add the fries and blanch until limp, yet
cooked and gently golden. This should take between 4-6
minutes. You can prevent the fries from sticking by gently
separating with kitchen tongs. It is important that you
maintain the oil heat at 325 degrees F.

8. Remove the fries from the pan and transfer to a kitchen paper towel plate.

9. Repeat the process until all of the potatoes are blanched.

10. Next, increase the heat to 375 degrees F.

11. Dredge the now blanched fries in the second mixing bowl of batter, evenly tossing to coat.

12. Still working in batches, cook the fries until golden and crisp, 1-2 minutes depending on the temperature fluctuation of the oil.

13. Transfer to a kitchen paper towel lined baking sheet, taste and season.

14. Serve.

Appetizers and Lite Bites

HHHHHHHHHHHHHHHHHHHHHHHHHHHHHHHHHHHHHHHH

Recipe 11: Spicy Beer Shrimp

Jazz up pan-fried shrimp with lager and spices for the ultimate appetizer or light bite to serve with pita bread, a green salad or rice.

Yield: 2

Preparation Time: 55mins

Ingredient List:

- 1 tablespoon olive oil
- 2 tablespoons butter
- ¼ cup onion (peeled, chopped)
- ⅔ cup lager
- 2 tablespoons tomato paste
- ¼ cup store-bought sweet chilli sauce
- 1 tablespoon fresh cilantro
- Few pinches cayenne pepper
- 1 pound shrimp (peeled, deveined, patted dry)

HHHHHHHHHHHHHHHHHHHHHHHHHHHHHHHHHHHHHH

Instructions:

1. In a large pan, heat the oil and butter until entirely melted.

2. Add the onion and cook for 5 minutes, until softened.

3. Pour in the lager and add the tomato paste, chili sauce, and cilantro and bring to boil. Sprinkle in a couple of pinches of cayenne.

4. When the mixture comes to boil, in a single layer add the shrimp to the pan and cook for 3 minutes. Turn the shrimp over and cook until the shrimp is pink, sufficiently cooked through and curled. This will take an additional 3 minutes.

5. Serve.

Recipe 12: Apricot and Horseradish Glazed Beer Roasted Ribs

Sweet jam and zesty horseradish make the perfect glaze for juicy ribs. The ideal make-ahead appetizer.

Yield: 6-8

Preparation Time: 2 days 3hours 30mins

Ingredient List:

- 1½ teaspoons salt (divided)
- 1½ teaspoons coarsely ground pepper (divided)
- 3 racks (8 pounds) baby back ribs (membranes removed)
- 2 (12 ounce) bottles beer
- 1 (12 ounce) jar apricot preserves
- ¼ cup prepared horseradish (drained)
- 2 tablespoons honey
- 1 teaspoon liquid smoke

HHHHHHHHHHHHHHHHHHHHHHHHHHHHHHHHHHH

Instructions:

1. Preheat the main oven to 325 degrees F.

2. Sprinkle 1 teaspoon of salt and 1 teaspoon of pepper over the ribs.

3. Transfer the ribs to a large roasting pan, bone side facing down.

4. Pour in the beer and cover.

5. Bake in the oven for 2-3 hours, until tender.

6. In the meantime, in a food blender, puree the apricot preserves along with the horseradish, honey, remaining seasoning and liquid smoke.

7. Drain the ribs.

8. Lay one rib rack on a large sheet of foil and brush with the puree.

9. Tightly wrap the ribs and repeat the process with the remaining ribs.

10. Transfer to the fridge for up to 48 hours.

11. When you are ready to serve. Preheat your grill to moderate heat.

12. Take the ribs out of the aluminum foil and grill for 10-15 minutes, until browned, while occasionally turning.

Recipe 13: Roasted Beer and Cauliflower Tacos with Homemade Lime Cilantro Coleslaw

Who needs meat when you can have lots of fresh veggies and spices? Vamp up a simple taco meal with Mexican beer, hot sauce, and lime. It's time to go south of the border!

Yield: 6

Preparation Time: 45mins

Ingredient List:

Slaw:

- ½ head green cabbage (cut into very thin 2" strips)
- 1 small carrot (cut into 2" matchsticks)
- 2 tablespoons freshly squeezed lime juice
- 2 tablespoons rice vinegar
- 1 teaspoon olive oil
- ⅛ teaspoons salt
- ⅓ cup cilantro (chopped)

Tacos:

- ¾ cup Mexican beer
- ¼ cup vegetable broth
- 1 tablespoon freshly squeezed lime juice
- 1½ teaspoons soy sauce
- 1½ tablespoons chipotle hot sauce
- 2 small cloves garlic (peeled, sliced)
- 1 head cauliflower (chopped into small florets)
- 1½ teaspoons chili powder
- 1 teaspoon smoked paprika
- ¼ teaspoons garlic powder
- Pinch of salt
- 1 tablespoon olive oil
- ½ yellow onion (peeled, chopped)
- 6 corn tortillas
- 1 ripe avocado (peeled, pitted, sliced)
- Tomato salsa (to serve)

HHHHHHHHHHHHHHHHHHHHHHHHHHHHHHHHHH

Instructions:

1. First, make the coleslaw.

2. In a bowl, combine the strips of cabbage, carrot matchsticks, fresh lime juice along with the rice vinegar, oil, and salt. Transfer to the fridge until you are ready to serve. Before you serve, fold in the chopped cilantro.

3. Next, make the tacos. Preheat the main oven to 400 degrees F.

4. In a pan over moderate heat, warm the beer, vegetable broth, fresh lime juice, soy sauce, chipotle sauce, and garlic. Stir well to combine. Add the cauliflower and simmer for 1-2 minutes. Drain.

5. In a mixing bowl, toss the chili powder with the paprika, garlic powder, pinch of salt and olive oil. Add the cauliflower florets and chopped onions and toss to combine.

6. Transfer to a rimmed baking sheet and bake until browned, stirring halfway through cooking, this will take around 20 minutes.

7. Assemble the tacos. Warm the tortillas.

8. Pile the cauliflower mixture on top, followed by the sliced avocado, coleslaw, and salsa.

Recipe 14: Beer Battered Chicken Strips

Chicken strips coated in a beer batter is a very simple dish to prepare and is sure to become an all-time family favorite snack or appetizer.

Yield: 6

Preparation Time: 30mins

Ingredient List:

- 1½ pounds skinless, boneless chicken breast halves
- 1½ cups all-purpose flour (divided)
- 1 teaspoon baking powder
- 2 medium eggs
- ½ cup beer (cold)
- 3 cups oil (to fry)

HHHHHHHHHHHHHHHHHHHHHHHHHHHHHHHHHHHHH

Instructions:

1. First, rinse the chicken. Pat dry with kitchen towel and cut into 1" strips.

2. In a bowl, combine 1 cup of flour with the baking powder.

3. Add the egg and pour in the beer, mix to combine.

4. Add the oil to a deep frying pan or skillet and heat to 375 degrees F.

5. Add the remaining flour to a bowl.

6. Dredge the chicken in the flour, then dip in the beer batter, making sure the chicken is evenly coated.

7. Fry the coated chicken strips, a few at a time in the oil, flipping over once until golden all over.

8. Remove from the pan and keep warm.

Recipe 15: Loaded Beer and Bacon Corn Chowder

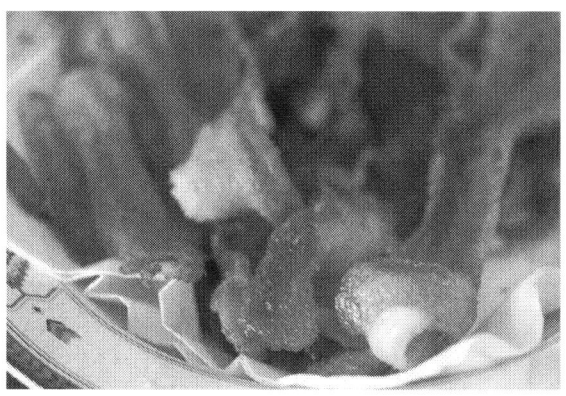

Creamy chowder is the perfect midweek snack or appetizer. It has lots of flavor and texture and is totally satisfying.

Yield: 4-6

Preparation Time: 45mins

Ingredient List:

- ½ pound bacon (cooked, crispy)
- ½ white onion (peeled, chopped)
- ½ cup carrots (peeled, chopped)
- 1 cup wheat beer
- 3 cups corn kernels
- 1 large sweet potato (peeled, diced)
- 2 cups chicken broth
- ½ cup half and half
- 1 teaspoon garlic powder
- 1 teaspoon chili powder
- 1 teaspoon salt
- ½ teaspoons smoked paprika
- 4 ounces Cheddar cheese (shredded)
- 5 green onions (chopped)
- 1 jalapeno (diced)

HHHHHHHHHHHHHHHHHHHHHHHHHHHHHHHHHHHH

Instructions:

1. In a pan, cook the bacon until crispy, cool and crumble.

2. Discard all but 2 tablespoons of bacon drippings from the pan.

3. Add the onions followed by the carrots to the pan and cook for 8-10 minutes, until caramelized and softened.

4. Pour in the beer and scrape the pot to deglaze.

5. Add 2 cups of corn, followed by the sweet potato, and chicken broth. Gently bring the mixture to simmer and cook the potatoes until fork tender.

6. With an immersion blender, blend until silky.

7. Add the half and half and stir to combine.

8. Add the remaining corn followed by the garlic powder, chili powder, salt, and paprika.

9. Cook over moderate heat, while stirring until sufficiently warm. Taste and adjust the seasoning and spices.

10. Ladle the chowder into cups or bowls.

11. Scatter with shredded cheese, onion, crumbled bacon, and diced jalapenos.

12. Enjoy.

Recipe 16: Buffalo Wings in Spicy Beer Marinade

All-time favorite appetizer gets a beer boost to deliver the best ever tasting buffalo wings. Perfect for a game night in or as a TV snack.

Yield: 12

Preparation Time: 1hour 30mins

Ingredient List:

- 1 tablespoon packed brown sugar
- 1 tablespoon sea salt
- 1 (12 ounce) bottle beer
- 2 pounds chicken wings
- 1½ teaspoons onion powder
- 1½ teaspoons garlic powder
- 1½ teaspoons paprika
- ¼ cup butter
- ¼ cup red pepper sauce
- Pepper sauce (to serve, optional)

HHHHHHHHHHHHHHHHHHHHHHHHHHHHHHHHHHHH

Instructions:

1. Preheat the main oven to 350 degrees F. Using aluminum foil, line a cookie sheet.

2. In a mixing bowl, beat the sugar with the salt. Pour in the beer and whisk to combine.

3. Add the chicken wings to the bowl, tossing gently to coat evenly.

4. Transfer to the fridge for half an hour.

5. In a zip lock bag, combine the onion powder with the garlic powder and paprika.

6. Remove the chicken from the brine and pat dry with kitchen paper. Discard the brine.

7. Add the chicken to the zip lock bag and toss to coat.

8. Remove the chicken from the bag, shaking off any excess seasoning and arrange on the cookie sheet.

9. In a pan, melt the butter.

10. Add the pepper sauce to the melted butter and bring to a simmer.

11. Pour the butter-pepper sauce over the chicken.

12. Bake in the preheated oven for 30-35 minutes, until the juices of the chicken run clear.

13. Serve with additional pepper sauce, if required.

Recipe 17: Irish Stout and Hazelnut Pate

Not only is this rich pate perfect for parties but also it makes an ideal edible gift. Serve with crusty French bread.

Yield: 8-12

Preparation Time: 8hours 40mins

Ingredient List:

- 14 ounces fatty pork breast (cut into large pieces)
- 11 ounces pork liver (cut into large pieces)
- 2 shallots (peeled, cut in half)
- 1 teaspoon pimento smoked paprika
- 25cl Irish stout
- 2 medium eggs
- ½ bunch parsley (chopped)
- 1¾ ounces hazelnuts (coarsely crushed)
- 4 teaspoons salt
- ¾ teaspoons pepper
- 2 bay leaves

Special equipment:

- 2 (500g) pate jars with airtight, resealable lids

HHHHHHHHHHHHHHHHHHHHHHHHHHHHHHHHHHHHHH

Instructions:

1. Add the pork, liver, and shallots to a dish followed by the paprika and stout. Mix to combine and set aside to marinate for 6 hours.

2. Drain the mixture and set aside 1 tablespoon of marinade.

3. Pass the mixture through a meat grinder.

4. Add the eggs followed by the parsley, hazelnuts, salt, and pepper and mix to incorporate thoroughly.

5. Fill the jars, while taking care to make sure the edges are clean. Place a bay leaf on top of the mixture and secure the lid.

6. Add the jars to your pressure cookers basket. Fill a ⅓ full with water. Chock the jars with tea towels, to avoid them colliding.

7. Cook for 50 minutes.

8. When the sterilization is completed, before opening the lid, remove the pressure cooker from the fire, without releasing the steam.

9. Allow to cool in order for the pressure to gently drop.

10. Wipe the jars, and store in a cool dark place.

Recipe 18: Chargrilled Lager Beer Glazed Scallops with Bacon

Nothing beats cooking outdoors, and you will love these tasty scallops with bacon and beer.

Yield: 2

Preparation Time: 40mins

Ingredient List:

- 12 fresh scallops (scrubbed, debearded)
- 2 tablespoons olive oil
- 1 tablespoon freshly squeezed lemon juice
- 1 tablespoon paprika
- Sea salt and black pepper
- 2 tablespoons butter
- 1 tablespoon garlic (peeled, minced)
- 1 tablespoon bacon (finely cut)
- 4 ounces German lager beer
- ¼ cup parsley (finely chopped)

HHHHHHHHHHHHHHHHHHHHHHHHHHHHHHHHHHHH

Instructions:

1. Using hardwood lump charcoal, light your fire and allow to burn for between 15-20 minutes, until white hot.

2. Disperse the charcoal evenly around the grill.

3. Approximately 10-12 minutes before cooking, preheat a skillet on the charcoal.

4. Season the cleaned scallops with olive oil, fresh lemon juice, paprika, sea salt, and pepper.

5. Add the butter followed by the garlic and bacon to the skillet and cook for 2 minutes.

6. Next, add the scallops to the skillet and cook for 2 minutes. Flip over and pour in the lager.

7. Simmer the scallops in the lager for an additional 2 minutes.

8. When the scallops are sufficiently cooked, remove from the skillet and sprinkle with parsley.

9. Enjoy.

Recipe 19: Hummus with Pale Ale

Add pizzazz to hummus with a healthy glug of pale ale.

Yield: 12

Preparation Time: 20mins

Ingredient List:

- 2 (15 ounce) cans chickpeas (rinsed, drained)
- 1 teaspoon freshly squeezed lemon juice
- 2 cloves garlic (peeled, minced)
- 1 teaspoon sesame seeds
- ¼ cup Indian pale ale
- 1 teaspoon coriander
- 1 teaspoon cumin
- ½ teaspoons salt
- ¼ teaspoons cayenne
- Pita bread or beer biscuits* (optional, to serve)

HHHHHHHHHHHHHHHHHHHHHHHHHHHHHHHHHHHH

Instructions:

1. In a food blender, puree the chickpeas, lemon juice, garlic, sesame seeds, pale ale, coriander, cumin, salt, and cayenne.

2. Remove from the blender, scraping down the sides and transfer to the fridge to chill slightly.

3. Serve with beer biscuits.*

*See the recipe on the next pages

Recipe 20: Cheddar and Beer Cheesecake

Catering for a crowd? Then this recipe is the one for you, a creamy, cheesy beer infused cheesecake.

Yield: 15-20

Preparation Time: 2hours

Ingredient List:

- 1½ cups crushed crackers
- ¼ cup margarine (melted)
- 1¾ cup sugar
- 6 ounces extra sharp Cheddar cheese (shredded)
- 4 (8 ounce) packs cream cheese (room temperature)
- 4 medium eggs
- 2 medium egg yolks
- ⅓ cup beer
- ¼ cup heavy cream

HHHHHHHHHHHHHHHHHHHHHHHHHHHHHHHHHHHH

Instructions:

1. Preheat the main oven to 300 degrees F.

2. In a bowl, combine the crushed crackers with the margarine and ¼ cup sugar. Mix to incorporate and firmly press the mixture into the base and halfway up a lightly buttered 12" springform pan.

3. In a second bowl, beat the cheddar and cream cheese along with the remaining sugar until light and fluffy.

4. One at a time add the eggs along with the egg yolks to the cheese, thoroughly beating between additions.

5. Pour in the beer and heavy cream and at low-speed beat to combine.

6. Transfer the mixture into the springform pan and bake in the oven for 2 hours.

7. Turn the oven off without removing the cheesecake, crack open the oven door and leave for half an hour.

8. Remove the cheesecake from the oven and allow to cool on a wire baking rack.

9. When cool transfer to the fridge, overnight.

10. When you are ready to serve, loosen the cake from the pan edges.

11. Remove the side of the springform pan and serve at room temperature.

Mains

HHHHHHHHHHHHHHHHHHHHHHHHHHHHHHHHHHHHHH

Recipe 21: Pop's Best Chilli

A hearty beef chilli is a filling and comforting meal.

Yield: 6-8

Preparation Time: 45mins

Ingredient List:

- 2 tablespoons olive oil
- 1 large onion (peeled, minced)
- 4 teaspoons garlic (peeled, minced)
- 1 cup carrots (minced)
- 1 pound ground beef
- 1 pound ground pork
- 1½ teaspoons cumin
- 2 tablespoons chilli powder
- ½ teaspoons cayenne pepper
- 1 tablespoon oregano
- 2 tablespoons brown sugar
- 2 (14 ounce) cans tomato sauce
- 2 (14 ounce) cans kidney beans (drained)
- 1 (12 ounce) can tomato paste
- 1½ teaspoons salt
- 1 (12 ounce) can beer
- Cooked white rice

HHHHHHHHHHHHHHHHHHHHHHHHHHHHHHHHHHHHH

Instructions:

1. Add the oil to a Dutch oven over moderate heat and add the onion, garlic, and carrot. Sauté for 5 minutes.

2. Add the meat and sauté until browned.

3. Stir in all remaining ingredients and simmer for half an hour until nice and thick.

4. Serve with cooked white rice.

Recipe 22: BBQ Pork Chops

A salty-sweet beer marinade with a refreshing ginger kick is the perfect partner to juicy grilled pork chops.

Yield: 4

Preparation Time: 8hours 20mins

Ingredient List:

- 2 tablespoons brown sugar
- ¼ cup soy sauce
- 1 cup beer
- 2 teaspoons fresh grated ginger
- 4 (¾" thick) bone-in pork chops

HHHHHHHHHHHHHHHHHHHHHHHHHHHHHHHHHHHHHH

Instructions:

1. First, make a marinade. Combine the sugar, soy sauce, beer, and ginger in a small bowl.

2. Add the pork chops to a large zip lock bag and pour in the marinade. Chill overnight.

3. Prepare a kettle-style grill with moderately hot coals.

4. Arrange the marinated pork chops directly on the grill, discarding the marinade. Cover and grill for several minutes, flipping once. A thermometer inserted into the meat should read 145 degrees F.

5. Allow to rest for a few minutes before serving.

Recipe 23: Pepperoni and Beer Pizza

Classic pepperoni pizza just got better thanks to a beer-infused tomato sauce.

Yield: 14

Preparation Time: 1hour

Ingredient List:

- 1 tablespoon olive oil
- 1 pound bacon (finely chopped)
- 1 garlic clove (peeled, minced)
- ½ pound pepperoni (finely chopped)
- 1 yellow onion (peeled, sliced)
- 4 ounces canned mushrooms
- 1 bell pepper (seeded, sliced)
- 1 cup beer
- 28 ounces canned tomatoes
- ½ teaspoons salt
- 1 teaspoon oregano
- ½ teaspoons thyme
- 2 readymade pizza dough bases
- 8 ounces mozzarella (shredded)

HHHHHHHHHHHHHHHHHHHHHHHHHHHHHHHHHHH

Instructions:

1. Preheat the main oven to 450 degrees F.

2. Place a skillet over moderate heat and pour in the oil. Add the bacon, garlic, and pepperoni, sauté until browned.

3. Add the onion, mushrooms, and bell pepper, cook for 5-6 minute.

4. In a second saucepan, add the beer and tomato sauce, stir to combine then add the mixture from the skillet.

5. Season with the salt and herbs and simmer for 15 minutes.

6. Spread the mixture over the pizza bases and sprinkle with plenty of shredded cheese.

7. Place in the oven and bake for just over 20 minutes until the cheese melts and the base is browned.

Recipe 24: Big Beef Brisket

A big beefy main is guaranteed to please all the family. Comfort food at its best.

Yield: 6

Preparation Time: 1hour 20mins

Ingredient List:

- 1 (2½-3 pound) beef brisket (sliced in half)
- ½ teaspoons black pepper
- 1 teaspoon celery salt
- ¼ teaspoons salt
- 1 onion (peeled, sliced)
- 2 teaspoons Worcestershire sauce
- 1 (12 ounce) bottle beer
- ¼ cup water
- 2 tablespoons cornstarch

HHHHHHHHHHHHHHHHHHHHHHHHHHHHHHHHHHHHHH

Instructions:

1. Rub the brisket halves with the black pepper and salts. Arrange the meat in a pressure cooker (6 quart) fatty side up. Scatter over the onion.

2. Stir together the Worcestershire sauce and beer. Pour over the meat in the pressure cooker. Secure the lid and close the vent. Cook for 70 minutes on high pressure.

3. When cooked, allow the pressure to release naturally to 10 minutes before quick releasing.

4. Take the beef out of the cooker and wrap in kitchen foil.

5. Strain the juices from the cooker into a pan over high heat and bring to a boil.

6. Combine the water and cornstarch in a bowl and pour into the sauce mixture. Stir to combine and cook until thick.

7. Serve the sauce poured over the beef.

Recipe 25: Meat-Free Stout Stew

A hearty and satisfying meat-free stew made with Irish stout and served with creamy mashed potatoes is perfect soul food.

Yield: 6

Preparation Time: 1hour 15mins

Ingredient List:

- 5 tablespoons olive oil
- 2 tablespoons soy sauce
- 14 ounces seitan (chopped)
- 1 yellow onion (peeled, finely chopped)
- 3 celery sticks (thinly sliced)
- 2 carrots (halved lengthwise, sliced)
- 2 potatoes (finely chopped)
- 3 garlic cloves (peeled, minced)
- 2 (12 ounce) bottle Irish stout
- 3 tablespoons brown sugar
- 2 tablespoons flour
- 1 tablespoon fresh thyme (chopped)
- Salt and pepper
- Mash potatoes (to serve)

HHHHHHHHHHHHHHHHHHHHHHHHHHHHHHHHHHHH

Instructions:

1. Over moderate to high heat, in a skillet, heat 2 tablespoons of oil and soy sauce.

2. Add the seitan and sauté until browned all over, for 4-6 minutes.

3. In a large pan over moderate to high heat, heat the remaining oil.

4. Add the onion, celery, carrots, potatoes, and garlic and sauté in hot oil for 3-5 minutes, until the onions are softened.

5. Turn the heat down to moderate and slowly stir the stout into the veggie mixture.

6. Stir the brown sugar, flour, chopped thyme, salt and pepper into the stout mixture. Add the seitan. Bring to simmer, turn the heat down to low and cook for 40-45 minutes until the stew thickens and reduces.

7. Serve.

Recipe 26: Fettuccine with Porter Beef Ragu

Rich porter is the perfect ingredient to a pasta sauce.

Yield: 6

Preparation Time: 1hour 20mins

Ingredient List:

- 1 pound ground sausage
- ½ cup carrot (chopped)
- ½ cup sweet onion (peeled, chopped)
- ⅓ cup sweet red pepper (chopped)
- ⅓ cup celery (chopped)
- 2 cloves garlic (peeled, minced)
- 1 (12 ounce) can porter beer
- 28 ounces canned tomatoes
- 1 tablespoon capers
- 2 tablespoons pimento stuffed olives (sliced)
- 1 cup mushrooms (peeled, sliced)
- 2 bay leaves
- 2 teaspoons basil
- ½ teaspoons caraway seeds
- ½ teaspoons black pepper
- 12 ounces fettuccine pasta

HHHHHHHHHHHHHHHHHHHHHHHHHHHHHHHHHHHH

Instructions:

1. Sauté the sausage in a skillet over moderate heat for several minutes until browned. Crumble and drain away any fat from the skillet.

2. Add the carrot, onion, red pepper, celery, and garlic. Cook for a few minutes before stirring in the beer, tomatoes, capers, olives, mushrooms, bay leaves, basil, caraway seeds, and black pepper. Bring the mixture to a boil then reduce to a simmer. Cook at a simmer for an hour, stirring occasionally. When cooked, discard the bay leaves.

3. When the sauce is almost ready, cook the fettuccine according to packet instructions. Drain and top with the sauce.

Recipe 27: Lamb and Ale Curry

Invite some friends around for a weekend meal, forget the take-out, and instead create this tasty curry.

Yield: 4

Preparation Time: 1hour 55mins

Ingredient List:

- 2 tablespoons peanut oil
- 1 red onion (peeled, sliced)
- 1" piece of fresh ginger (peeled, chopped)
- 3 garlic cloves (peeled, finely chopped)
- 1 teaspoon fresh turmeric (chopped)
- 1 red chilli (finely sliced)
- 1 teaspoon cardamom seeds
- 1 teaspoon lemongrass powder
- 2 tablespoons red curry paste
- 1 (9 ounce) boneless, lamb leg (cut into 1 ½ "chunks)
- 4½ ounces plain yoghurt
- 1 (12 ounce) bottle of 8% ale
- 3 potatoes (peeled, each cut into 6 pieces)
- 1 large handful fresh cilantro (chopped, divided)
- 16 sugar snap peas (topped, tailed)
- 16 green beans (topped, tailed)
- Rice (to serve)

HHHHHHHHHHHHHHHHHHHHHHHHHHHHHHHHHHHH

Instructions:

1. Preheat the main oven to 325 degrees F.

2. Over moderate heat, heat the oil in a flameproof baking dish.

3. Add the onion and cook while frequently stirring, until the onion begins to caramelize.

4. Add the ginger along with the garlic, turmeric, and chilli and cook, while stirring for 4-5 minutes.

5. Add the cardamom seeds and lemongrass powder and stir for 2-3 minutes more.

6. Stir in the curry paste, cooking until fragrant, before adding the pieces of lamb. Stir thoroughly to ensure that all the lamb is coated.

7. Stir in the yogurt and bring to gentle simmer.

8. Pour in the beer, stirring thoroughly to incorporate. Return to simmer.

9. Place the lid on the baking dish and transfer to the oven to bake for 45 minutes.

10. Remove the lid from the dish and stir in the potato along with 2 tablespoons of cilantro.

11. Replace the lid and bake for an additional 30-40 minutes, or until the meat is tender.

12. Add the peas and beans to the dish and cook, while covered for 5 minutes.

13. When you are ready to serve, stir the remaining cilantro through and enjoy with rice.

Recipe 28: German Beer Brats

Juicy brats braised in beer and garlic are perfect for serving in buns with braised onions at your next garden party or cookout.

Yield: 6

Preparation Time: 30mins

Ingredient List:

- 1 teaspoon red pepper (crushed)
- 1 teaspoon house seasoning
- 4 garlic cloves (peeled, crushed)
- 1 onion (peeled, thinly sliced)
- 2 (12 ounce) cans beer
- 6 bratwurst links

HHHHHHHHHHHHHHHHHHHHHHHHHHHHHHHHHHHHHH

Instructions:

1. Add the crushed red pepper, house seasoning, crushed garlic, onion, and beer to a Dutch oven over moderate heat. Stir well and add the bratwurst.

2. Bring the mixture to a boil then turn down to a simmer for 10 minutes.

3. Transfer the brats to a grill and cook for 5 minutes each side over moderate heat.

4. Serve in buns topped with some cooked onion from the pan.

Recipe 29: Jamaican Jerk Chicken

Serve this Caribbean-inspired main course with rice and peas.

Yield: 4-6

Preparation Time: 8hours 50mins

Ingredient List:

Marinade:

- 1 tablespoon English mustard
- 1 tablespoon red wine vinegar
- Zest and juice of 2 medium limes
- 3 tablespoons brown sugar
- 2-3 Habanero chilies (deseeded)
- 5 cloves garlic (peeled)
- 5 spring onions
- Few sprigs fresh thyme
- 1 tablespoon jerk seasoning
- 3 ½ ounces lager
- ½ teaspoons sea salt

Chicken:

- 1 (4 pound) chicken (spatchcocked)
- Groundnut oil (to rub)
- Rice (to serve)
- Peas (to serve)

HHHHHHHHHHHHHHHHHHHHHHHHHHHHHHHHHHHH

Instructions:

1. To make the marinade. Add the mustard, vinegar, lime zest and juice, brown sugar, chilies, garlic, onions, thyme, jerk seasoning, lager and sea salt in a food blender and process until entirely smooth.

2. Coat the chicken with the marinade, cover and allow to marinate in the refrigerator, overnight.

3. Preheat the main oven to 400 degrees F.

4. Wipe off any excess marinade from the chicken and rub with oil.

5. Either barbecue or griddle the chicken with breast side facing down, until the skin begins to char and turns golden. Take care not to allow the chicken to burn.

6. Place the chicken on a baking pan and roast in the oven for 35 minutes, until the juices run clear and the chicken is sufficiently cooked.

7. Remove the chicken from the oven and allow to rest for several minutes, before carving and serving with rice and peas.

Recipe 30: Irish Stout and Venison Pie

Celebrate National Beer Day with this winning combination of juicy venison and Irish stout and enjoy a flavorful pie from the Emerald Isle.

Yield: 6-8

Preparation Time: 1hour 50mins

Ingredient List:

- 2 rashers streaky bacon (diced)
- 1 clove garlic (peeled, minced)
- 2 large onions (peeled, diced)
- Flour
- 4½ pounds venison (diced into ¾" pieces)
- Beef stock
- 2 large carrots (diced)
- 2 large potatoes (diced)
- 1 (15 ounce) can Irish stout beer
- 1 tablespoon cornflour combined with 1 tablespoon water (optional)
- 1 sheet ready-made puff pastry

HHHHHHHHHHHHHHHHHHHHHHHHHHHHHHHHHHH

Instructions:

1. In a dry, deep-sided frying pan, fry the bacon to render the bacon fat. Remove the bacon from the pan and use for another purpose. Leave the bacon fat in the pan.

2. Using the same pan, sauté the garlic along with the onions in the bacon fat until caramelized. Remove and put aside.

3. Add flour to a shallow dish.

4. Dredge the pieces of venison in the flour, making sure it is evenly coated and add to the frying pan, cooking until browned. Return the garlic along with the caramelized onions to the frying pan.

5. Pour in a sufficient amount of beef stock to cover the ingredients while stirring to incorporate. Bring to a gentle simmer and simmer for 1 hour.

6. Add the carrots followed by the potatoes and simmer until fork tender. Remove the pan from the heat and pour in the Irish stout. Stir to combine.

7. If needed, thicken the gravy with a small amount of cornflour combined with a drop or two of water.

8. Transfer the mixture to a baking dish and cover with the sheet of prepared puff pastry. With a knife make a few slits in the top of the pie.

9. Bake in the main oven at 350 degrees F, for 15-20 minutes or until the pastry is puffed and golden.

10. Serve.

Desserts and Sweets

HHHHHHHHHHHHHHHHHHHHHHHHHHHHHHHHHHHHH

Recipe 31: Spicy Jalapeno Berry Popsicles

If you love trying daring new flavor combinations, then you will love these fruity, fiery and boozy popsicles.

Yield: N/A*

Preparation Time: 8hours 10mins

Ingredient List:

- 1 pound fresh strawberries
- 1-2 jalapeno peppers (seeded)
- ½ pound fresh raspberries
- 12 ounces ale
- ¼ cup white sugar

HHHHHHHHHHHHHHHHHHHHHHHHHHHHHHHHHHHH

Instructions:

1. Add the strawberries, jalapenos, raspberries, ale, and white sugar to a blender and blitz until combined.

2. Pour the mixture into your chosen popsicle mold. Freeze overnight until solid.

*The number of popsicles will depend on the size of your molds

Recipe 32: Beeramisu

The classic Italian dessert with a beer twist, the perfect end to any meal.

Yield: 4

Preparation Time: 12hours 15mins

Ingredient List:

- 3 tablespoons white sugar
- ¼ cup mascarpone (at room temperature)
- 3 tablespoons heavy whipping cream
- ½ cup stout
- 9 ladyfinger biscuits
- Cocoa powder (to dust)

HHHHHHHHHHHHHHHHHHHHHHHHHHHHHHHHHHH

Instructions:

1. Whisk together the sugar and mascarpone until combined.

2. Using an electric mixer, whip up the whipping cream until it can hold stiff peaks.

3. Fold the cream into the mascarpone mixture until incorporated.

4. Pour the stout into a wide dish.

5. Soak the ladyfinger biscuits in the stout for a few minutes each side. Don't oversoak.

6. Take 4 small cups/dishes, divide the soaked biscuits between the dishes, arranging in a single layer in the base of the dishes.

7. Spoon the mascarpone mixture on top of the biscuits and dust with cocoa powder.

8. Chill for at least 12 hours before serving.

Recipe 33: Spiced Cherry Beer Bundt

A delicious bundt cake flavored with aromatic spices, beer and studded with chewy dried cherries.

Yield: 12

Preparation Time: 1hour 40mins

Ingredient List:

- 2 teaspoons bicarb of soda
- 3 cups flour
- Pinch salt
- 2 teaspoons cinnamon
- 2 teaspoons allspice
- ½ teaspoons cloves
- 2 cups brown sugar
- 1 cup salted butter
- 2 medium eggs
- 2 cups beer
- 1 cup chopped dried cherries
- 1 cup nuts (chopped)

HHHHHHHHHHHHHHHHHHHHHHHHHHHHHHHHHHHH

Instructions:

1. Preheat the main oven to 350 degrees F. Grease a large bundt tin and set to one side.

2. Combine the bicarb of soda, flour, salt, and spices in a bowl.

3. In a second bowl, whisk together the sugar and butter. When combined, whisk in the eggs.

4. Mix the dry ingredients into the wet ingredients a little at a time, alternating with splashes of beer.

5. Fold the cherries and chopped nuts into the batter.

6. Pour the batter into the cake tin and place in the oven for 60 minutes.

7. Allow to cool in the tin before removing and allowing to cool completely.

Recipe 34: Brown Sugar Beer Cookies

Soft and chewy cookies that melt in the mouth are a delicious sweet snack with a cold glass of milk.

Yield: 24

Preparation Time: 30mins

Ingredient List:

- Nonstick spray
- 1¼ cups brown sugar
- ¾ cup unsalted butter (at room temperature)
- Yolk of 1 large egg
- ½ teaspoons vanilla essence
- ⅓ cup brown ale
- 1¼ teaspoons bicarb of soda
- 1 cup bread flour
- 1¼ cups all-purpose flour
- ½ teaspoons salt
- 1 teaspoon baking powder
- ¼ teaspoons cinnamon
- 1 teaspoon cornstarch

HHHHHHHHHHHHHHHHHHHHHHHHHHHHHHHHHHH

Instructions:

1. Preheat the main oven to 325 degrees F.

2. Spritz 2 cookie sheets with nonstick spray and set to one side.

3. Using an electric mixer, whisk together the sugar and butter until fluffy. Mix in the yolk, vanilla essence and brown ale.

4. In a second bowl, combine the bicarb of soda, flours, salt, baking powder, cinnamon, and cornstarch. Fold this dry mixture into the wet mixture until combined.

5. Drop tablespoonfuls of the dough onto the cookie sheets.

6. Place in the oven and bake for 12-13 minutes. Allow to completely cool before serving.

Recipe 35: Shortbread Topped with Beer and Blackberry Jam

Rich and buttery shortbread topped with a tangy beer and blackberry fruit jam is a match made in heaven.

Yield: 9

Preparation Time: 3hours 30mins

Ingredient List:

Shortbread:

- ⅓ cup confectioner's sugar
- 1 cup all-purpose flour
- ½ teaspoons kosher salt
- 1 teaspoon vanilla essence
- 6 tablespoons butter (chopped)

Jam Topping:

- 1 cup wild ale
- 1 pound fresh blackberries
- 1 cup confectioner's sugar

HHHHHHHHHHHHHHHHHHHHHHHHHHHHHHHHHHHH

Instructions:

1. Preheat the main oven to 350 degrees F.

2. First, make the shortbread. Combine the confectioner's sugar, flour, and salt in a food processor and pulse to bring together.

3. Add the vanilla essence and butter to the processor and pulse again to form a dough.

4. Line an 8" square dish with parchment. Press the shortbread dough evenly into the base of the dish.

5. Place in the oven and bake for approximately 20 minutes until pale golden. Allow to cool.

6. Next, make the jam topping. To a saucepan over moderately high heat, add the ale, blackberries, and confectioner's sugar. Bring to a boil and cook for 10-12 minutes until thick. Stir occasionally.

7. Spoon the mixture over the cooked shortbread and chill for 2-3 hours before slicing and serving.

Recipe 36: Caramel Apple Beer Loaf

A moist and delicious loaf made with Belgian wheat beer with an indulgent caramel apple sauce. The ultimate afternoon treat.

Yield: 8

Preparation Time: 1hour 30mins

Ingredient List:

- Caramel Sauce:
- 2 tablespoons butter (chopped)
- 2 tablespoons water
- ¾ cup white sugar

Bread:

- 3 tablespoons white sugar
- 3 cups flour
- ½ teaspoons kosher salt
- 2½ teaspoons baking powder
- ¼ cup walnuts (chopped)
- 1½ cups peeled, chopped green apple
- ½ teaspoons cinnamon
- 12 ounces Belgian wheat beer
- 4 tablespoons butter (melted)

HHHHHHHHHHHHHHHHHHHHHHHHHHHHHHHHHHHH

Instructions:

1. Preheat the main oven to 350 degrees F.

2. First, make the sauce. Add the butter, water, and sugar to a saucepan over high heat and stir until the butter melts.

3. Bring the mixture to a boil for 5 minutes, do not stir. The mixture should be an amber color.

4. Next, prepare the bread. Combine the sugar, flour, salt, baking powder, walnuts, chopped apple, and cinnamon.

5. Stir the beer and melted butter into the dry ingredients until the batter comes together. Transfer to a loaf tin. Pour over the prepared sauce.

6. Place in the oven and bake for approximately 50 minutes until set.

7. Allow to cool before slicing and serving.

Recipe 37: Salted Pretzel Caramels

Beer flavored caramel candies with a crunchy salted pretzel topping make a delicious food gift for family and friends.

Yield: 28

Preparation Time: 40mins

Ingredient List:

- 2 cups brown sugar
- 1 cup butter
- 12 ounces beer
- 1 (14 ounce) can sweetened condensed milk
- 1 cup corn syrup
- 1 teaspoon vanilla essence
- Salted pretzels (crushed)

HHHHHHHHHHHHHHHHHHHHHHHHHHHHHHHHHHHH

Instructions:

1. Line a 13x9" tin with parchment and set to one side.

2. In a saucepan over moderate heat, melt together the sugar and butter. While stirring, pour in the beer, followed by the condensed milk and corn syrup until combined.

3. Continue to cook and stir until the mixture reaches 240 degrees F. Take off the heat and mix in the vanilla essence.

4. Pour the caramel mixture into the pan and sprinkle with the crushed pretzels.

5. Allow to cool completely until firm. Slice into bite-size pieces.

Recipe 38: Chocolate Stout Ice Cream

Chocolate stout beer has a deep, malty flavor and makes for a super smooth and indulgent ice cream.

Yield: 6

Preparation Time: 8hours 15mins

Ingredient List:

- 1 (14 ounce) can sweetened condensed milk
- 1 pint heavy whipping cream
- ⅓ cup chocolate-flavored stout beer
- 1 tablespoon vanilla essence
- Toffee bits

HHHHHHHHHHHHHHHHHHHHHHHHHHHHHHHHHHHHHH

Instructions:

1. Whisk together the condensed milk, cream, beer, and vanilla essence using an electric mixer until the mixture can hold stiff peaks.

2. Transfer the mixture to a loaf tin and freeze overnight.

3. When ready to serve, scoop into bowls and sprinkle with toffee bits.

Recipe 39: Irish Stout Mousse Cups

Rich chocolate mousse cups topped with whip cream look and taste like your favorite Irish stout beer.

Yield: 2

Preparation Time: 2hours 20mins

Ingredient List:

- ¾ cup whipping cream
- ¼ cup Irish stout beer
- 4 ounces semisweet chocolate (roughly chopped)
- 1 tablespoon + 1 teaspoon white sugar
- 2 medium eggs (separated)
- Dark chocolate (grated)

HHHHHHHHHHHHHHHHHHHHHHHHHHHHHHHHHHHHH

Instructions:

1. Add a ¼ cup of cream and all of the beer to a saucepan over moderate heat. Cook until the mixture begins to bubble. Take off the heat, add the chopped chocolate and whisk well until the chocolate completely melts. Set to one side.

2. In a separate bowl, whisk 1 tablespoon of white sugar and the yolks together until combined. Add a little of the melted chocolate mixture to the yolks and stir to combine. Add this mixture to the original melted chocolate mixture and set to one side to cool for 20 minutes.

3. Whip up the egg whites until they can hold stiff peaks. Fold the egg whites into the cool chocolate mixture. Divide between two short glasses. Chill for a couple of hours.

4. Whip up the remaining cream until fluffy and thick. Whisk in the sugar until combined.

5. Spoon the cream on top of the chilled mousses to resemble a pint. Sprinkle with grated chocolate.

Recipe 40: Frosted Dark Beer Brownies

Fudgy, rich brownies and a fluffy buttercream frosting are a decadent dessert for the one you love.

Yield: 8

Preparation Time: 1hour 30mins

Ingredient List:

Brownies:

- 1 cup stout beer
- ½ cup + 1 tablespoon unsweetened cocoa powder
- 8 tablespoons unsalted butter
- 2 ounces bitter chocolate (roughly chopped)
- 1 cup + 2 tablespoons white sugar
- 1 teaspoon vanilla essence
- White of 1 large egg
- ¼ teaspoons salt
- ½ cup all-purpose flour

Frosting:

- 1 cup confectioner's sugar
- 6 tablespoons unsalted butter (at room temperature)

HHHHHHHHHHHHHHHHHHHHHHHHHHHHHHHHHHH

Instructions:

1. First, make the brownies. Bring the beer to a boil in a saucepan over moderately high heat for approximately 20 minutes, until it reduces to a ⅓ cup.

2. Preheat the main oven to 325 degrees F. Cover a loaf tin with parchment and set to one side.

3. Combine the cocoa powder, butter, chopped chocolate, and sugar in a bowl. Pop in the microwave for 60 seconds, removing halfway through to stir well. Allow to cool.

4. Stir 4 tablespoons of the thickened beer mixture into the melted chocolate along with the vanilla, egg white, and salt until combined.

5. Fold the flour into the mixture until incorporated.

6. Transfer the batter to the loaf tin and place in the oven for just over 40 minutes. Allow to completely cool.

7. In the meantime, make the frosting. Using an electric whisk, beat together the confectioner's sugar and butter until fluffy.

8. Smooth the frosting over the cooled brownies and slice.

About the Author

Angel Burns learned to cook when she worked in the local seafood restaurant near her home in Hyannis Port in Massachusetts as a teenager. The head chef took Angel under his wing and taught the young woman the tricks of the trade for cooking seafood. The skills she had learned at a young age helped her get accepted into Boston University's Culinary Program where she also minored in business administration.

Summers off from school meant working at the same restaurant but when Angel's mentor and friend retired as head chef, she took over after graduation and created classic and new dishes that delighted the diners. The restaurant flourished under Angel's culinary creativity and one customer developed more than an appreciation for Angel's food. Several months after taking over the position, the young woman met her future husband at work and they have been inseparable ever since. They still live in Hyannis Port with their two children and a cocker spaniel named Buddy.

Angel Burns turned her passion for cooking and her business acumen into a thriving e-book business. She has authored several successful books on cooking different types of dishes using simple ingredients for novices and experienced chefs alike. She is still head chef in Hyannis Port and says she will probably never leave!

♥ ♭ ♥ ♥ ♥ ♥ ♥ ♥ ♭ ♥ ♥ ♥ ♥ ♥ ♥ ♥ ♭ ♥ ♥ ♥ ♥ ♥ ♥ ♥

Author's Afterthoughts

With so many books out there to choose from, I want to thank you for choosing this one and taking precious time out of your life to buy and read my work. Readers like you are the reason I take such passion in creating these books.

It is with gratitude and humility that I express how honored I am to become a part of your life and I hope that you take the same pleasure in reading this book as I did in writing it.

Can I ask one small favour? I ask that you write an honest and open review on Amazon of what you thought of the book. This will help other readers make an informed choice on whether to buy this book.

My sincerest thanks,

Angel Burns

If you want to be the first to know about news, new books, events and giveaways, subscribe to my newsletter by clicking the link below

https://angel-burns.gr8.com

or Scan QR-code

Printed in Great Britain
by Amazon